Desert Icons

Adult Coloring Book

Hand Drawn by Suzanne Wood Artist/Illustrator

Suzannewoodarts.com

ISBN: 978-1-7978-1893-1

Desert Icons

Colored By: _______________________________

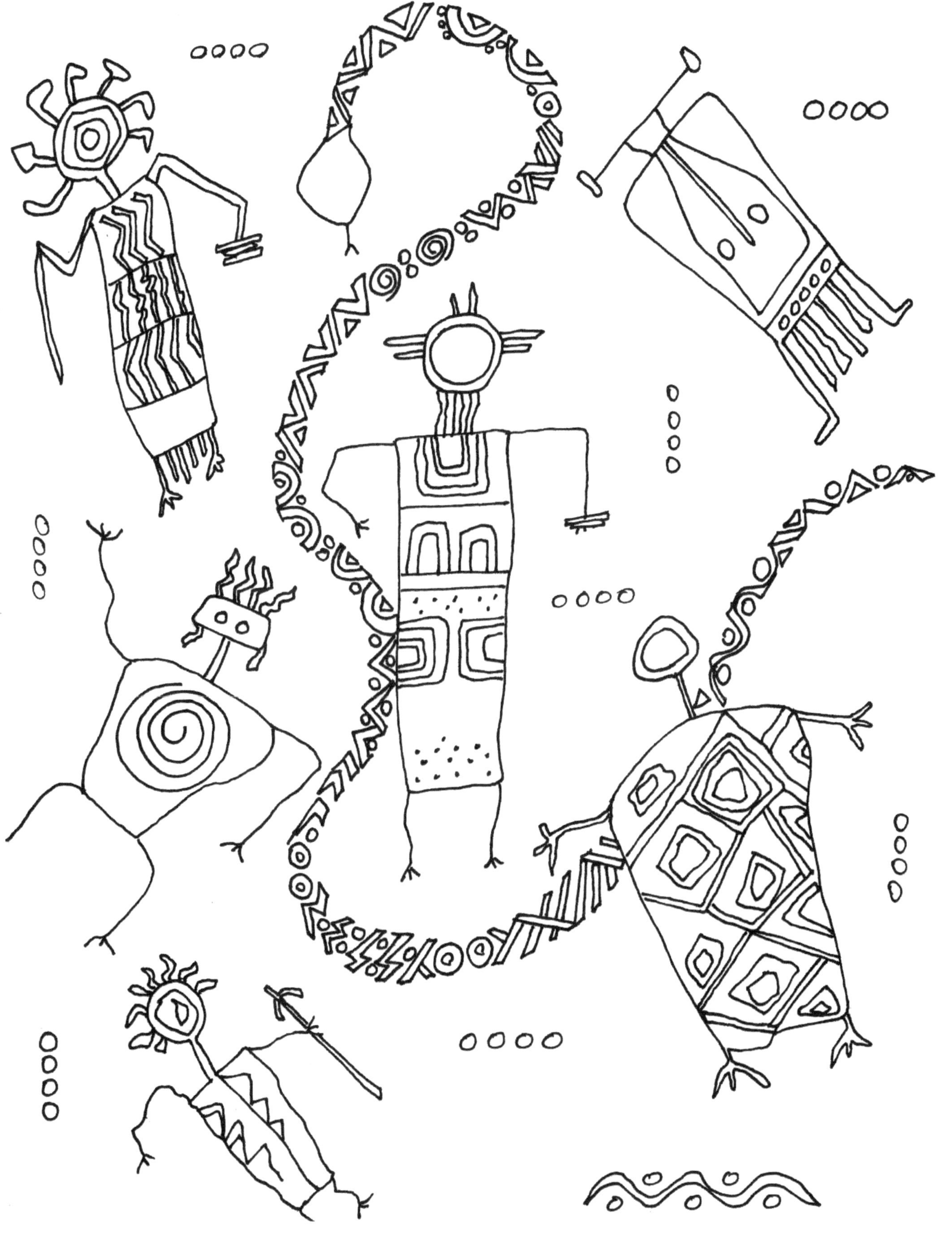

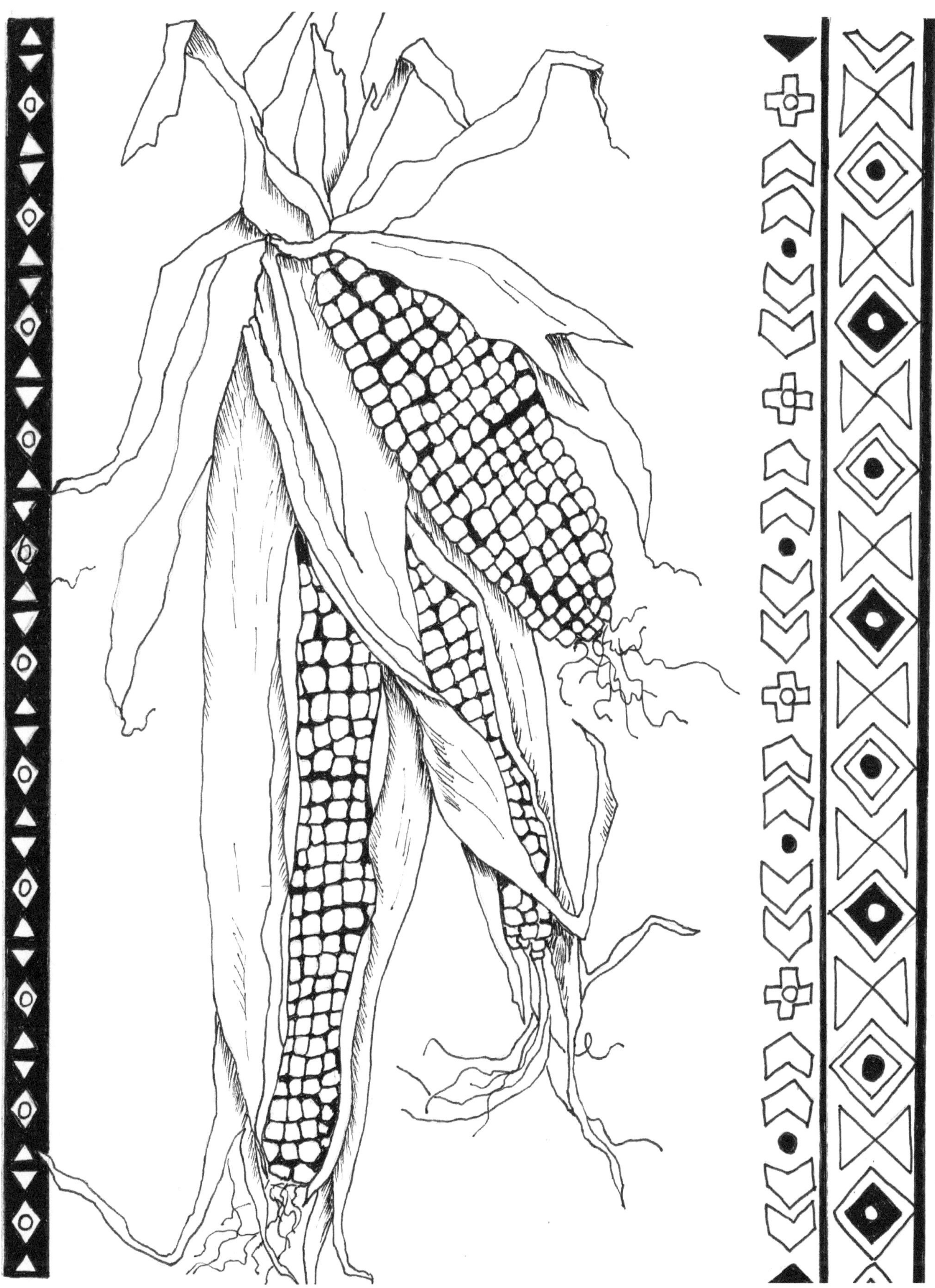

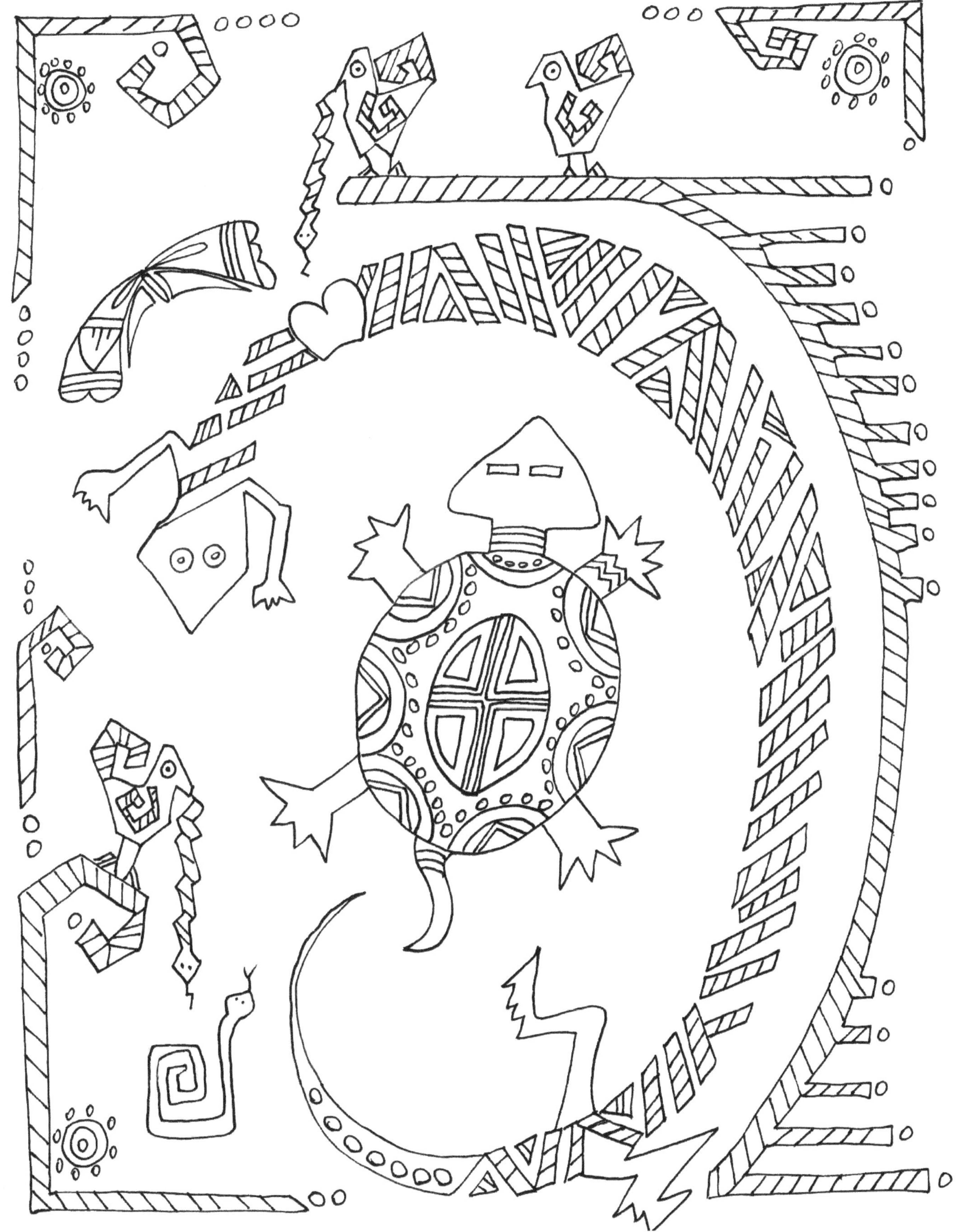

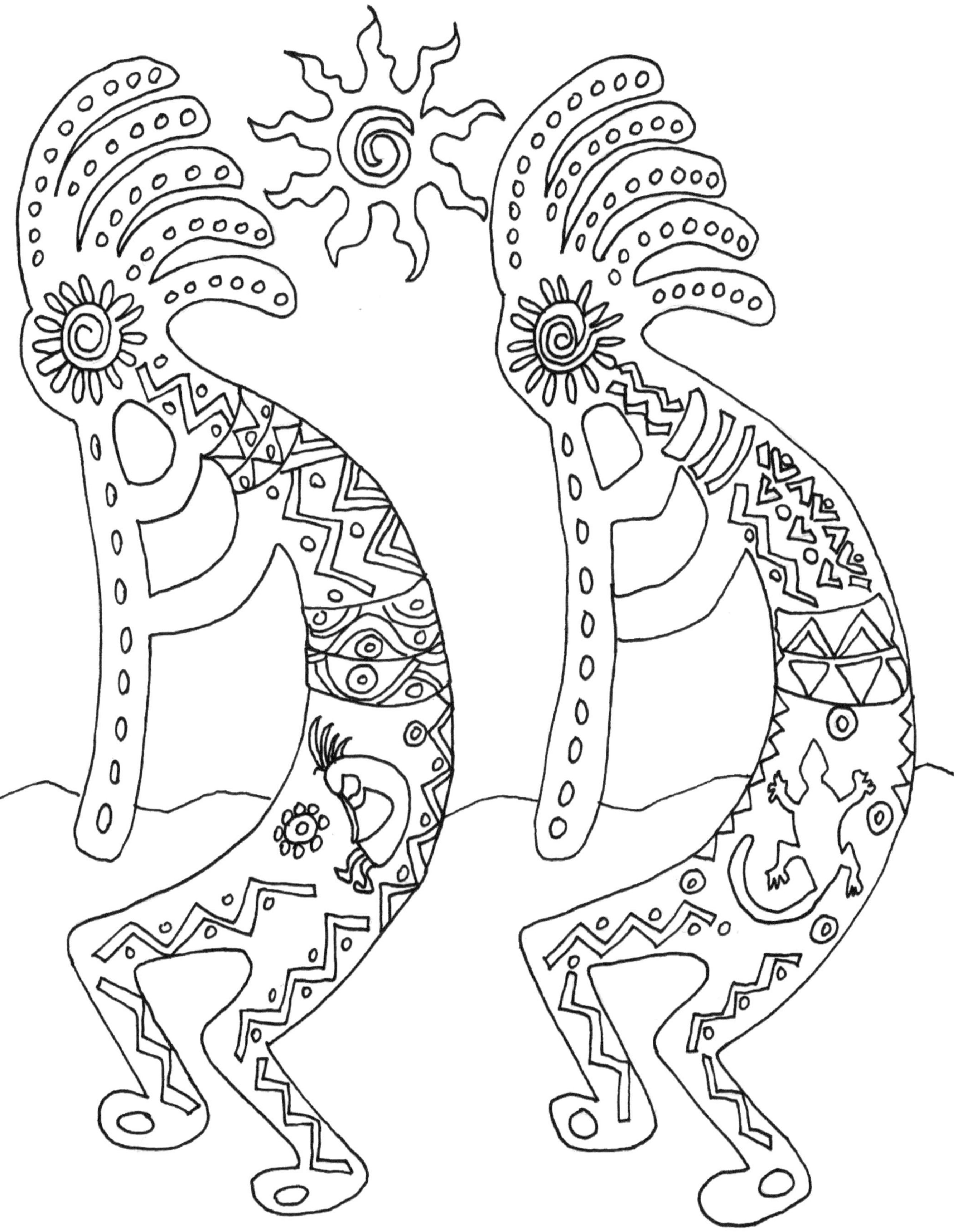

Other Books by this Author:

www.amazon.com/author/woodsuzanne

Adult Coloring Books

Odd Birds

Ancient Beasts

Chairs

Birds and Bees, Flowers and Trees

Children's Coloring Book

Super Silly Birds

For Kids ages 8 to 12

Gardening Book

Winter Gardening Guide

Available in Paperback and Kindle

Thank you for your Patronage.